A Pirate's Life for Me!

A Day Aboard a Pirate Ship

Julie Thompson and Brownie Macintosh

Illustrated by Patrick O'Brien

Charlesbridge

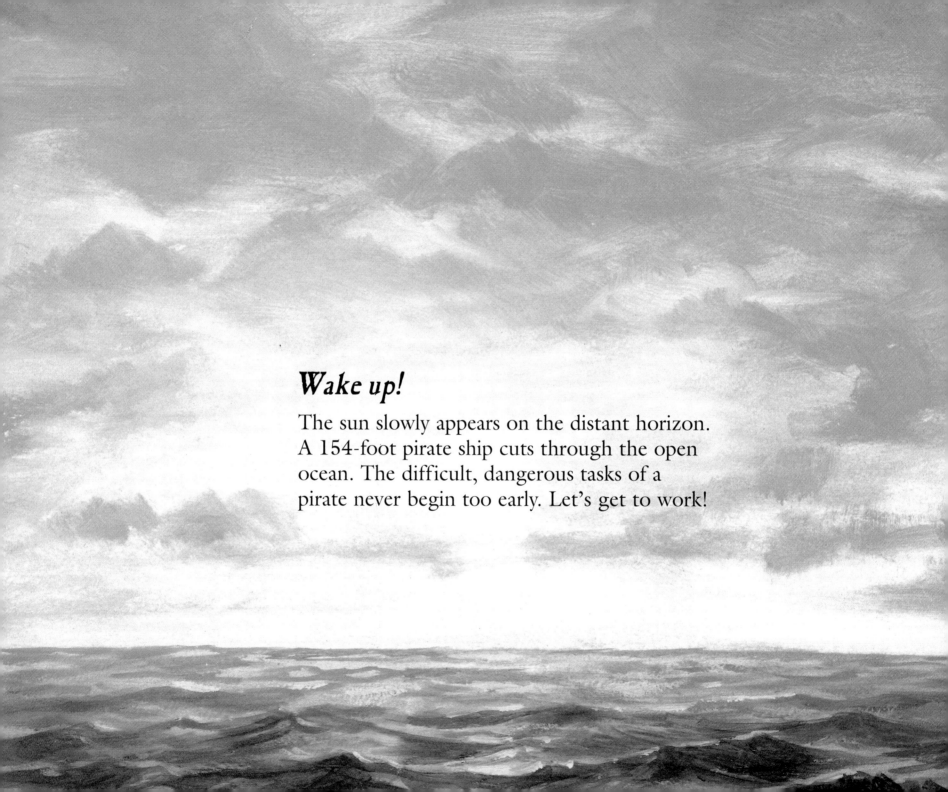

Wake up!

The sun slowly appears on the distant horizon. A 154-foot pirate ship cuts through the open ocean. The difficult, dangerous tasks of a pirate never begin too early. Let's get to work!

Ahoy, mateys!

Last night, many of the pirates slept in hammocks on the ship's dark, smelly lower deck. They were packed together among barrels of water, extra lines, sails, firewood, and salted meat. Most pirates do not have houses— the ship is their home.

Some pirates wear their hair in long braids. Others shave their heads to keep their hair free of lice and bugs.

Most pirates wear gold earrings. If they are thrown from the ship in a storm and their bodies wash up on land, the earrings will be worth enough to pay for their burials! Some pirates wear earrings as a sign that they have survived a shipwreck.

All hands on deck!

The pirates on the night watch have been awake for hours already, sailing through the darkness. Sleepily, they greet their crewmates. All pirates on board have important jobs to do. Several of them man the pumps. Others haul on the halyards. "Look out!" shouts one pirate. "There's a storm a-comin' our way!" The pirates quickly move their tools and extra lines below decks, so the big waves will not wash them overboard.

Men overboard!

What a storm! Two pirates fall overboard—a fine meal for hungry sharks. The wind-powered ship cannot turn around to rescue them, and most pirates never learn how to swim.

Even in good weather, the ship is constantly taking on seawater. In a storm, it might sink. A pirate's life is full of danger!

Patch the sails!

When the storm is over, there are several repairs to make. The quartermaster makes sure everyone is working hard. Many pirates are busy sewing up the huge canvas sails that were torn to shreds in the squall.

Others take strands of tarred rope, or oakum, and press them between the ship's wooden planks to stop leaks that opened up in the storm.

The ship's cook is preparing a usual midday meal: moldy biscuits and boiled salt beef.

Stay on course!

A storm can easily blow the ship miles off course. The ship's navigator and his mate use a cross-staff or a quadrant to find out where the ship is now. By measuring the angle of the sun over the horizon, they can tell the ship's latitude. Their compass shows them which way they are going. The navigator checks a chart to make sure they are still headed for the pirates' secret island hideout.

A few pirates have pets. The cook has a cat. The quartermaster has a monkey, who is always stealing food. The captain has a parrot he got when the ship stopped in South America. There are unwanted animals on board as well—rats!

Man the lookout!

Nearly one hundred feet in the air, perched on a crow's nest, one sailor scans the horizon with a spyglass. He is looking for a Spanish galleon to attack and rob. Pirates take valuable cargo, such as gold, silver, gems, weapons, tobacco, timber, spices, and silks. They will steal anything they can use or sell.

Climb the ratlines!

Pirates carefully climb the main ratlines. The sailors adjust the rigging and yards. The sails snap sharply as they catch a brisk wind. The ship moves quickly now, at about twelve miles per hour over rough, choppy waves.

A merry life!

After many of their jobs are done, the pirates can have some fun. Some pirates play games such as cards and checkers. Some carve wood or practice target shooting. Others sing or dance the hornpipe. A lucky crew has a pirate who knows how to play a fife, fiddle, or drum. But soon, the pirates see a chance to attack.

Hoist the Jolly Roger!

Using a spyglass, a sharp-eyed pirate catches a glimpse of a large merchant ship loaded with treasure. The pirate captain orders his crew to sail toward it. He yells, "Pirates, prepare for battle. Hoist the Jolly Roger!" This flag strikes fear into the hearts of merchant sailors. It means "Give up your cargo or die!"

Load the cannons!

The master gunner watches carefully as his crew rushes to get the cannons ready for battle. Powder monkeys give gunpowder and cannonballs to the burly gunners. The gunners aim the heavy cannons at the merchant's masts. The pirates brandish their cutlasses, muskets, and huge, long-handled boarding axes. The captain orders his crew to ready their grappling hooks and stinkpots.

Ready, Aim, Fire!

BOOM! The cannons fire a warning shot in front of the other ship. Will the merchant crew fight to protect their treasures or surrender to save their lives? The pirates quickly sail up alongside the merchant ship. They lift their weapons above their heads, blow horns, beat loudly on drums, and yell. The pirate captain, armed with a set of pistols, directs the attack. "An extra share of loot," he shouts, "for the first pirate aboard!"

Board and plunder!

A few strong pirates throw sharp metal grappling hooks into the merchant ship's rigging. The pirates cheer and howl as they climb aboard the merchant ship—the terrified crew does not dare fight back.

Working together quickly, the pirates take chests of sugar, gold, and valuable spices. Some pirates head for the hold to plunder the ship's stores of food and drink.

The pirate captain calls out to the merchant crew, "Look at you, slaving away for a rich merchant captain. Which of you has the courage to join us and live the free life of a pirate?"

The pirate ship always needs new recruits to replace those who fall overboard or are killed. The pirates cheer as many of the sailors cross to the pirate ship.

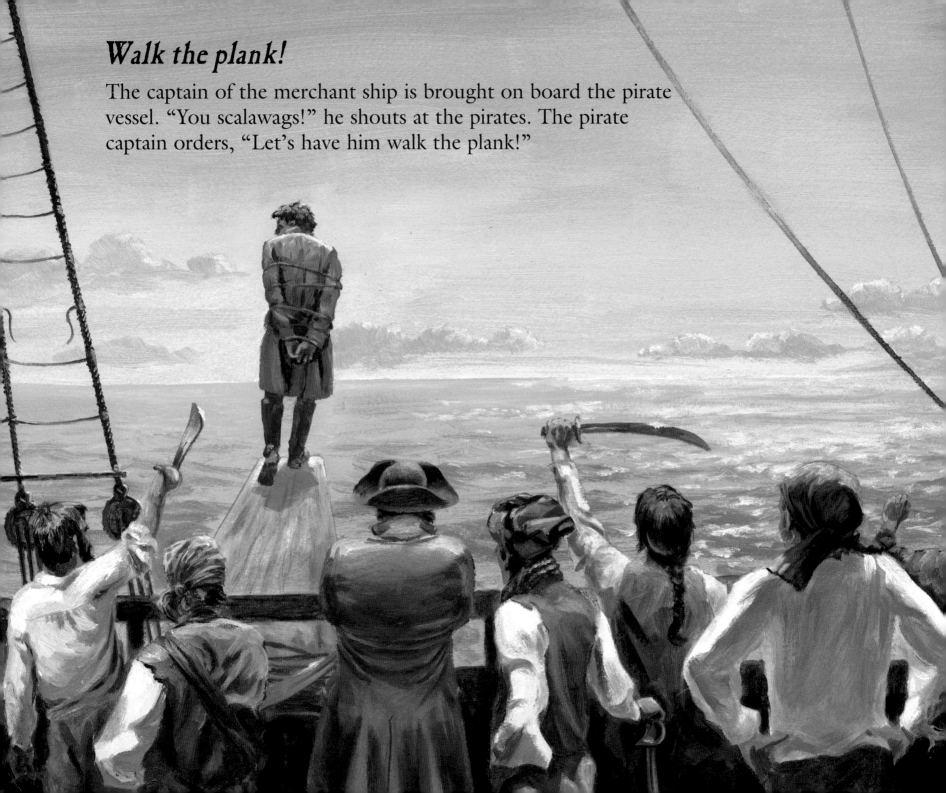

Walk the plank!

The captain of the merchant ship is brought on board the pirate vessel. "You scalawags!" he shouts at the pirates. The pirate captain orders, "Let's have him walk the plank!"

Pirate meeting!

The pirates sail to their hideout: a small, deserted island. There they gather together on the deck to divide up the loot. Each pirate gets an equal share. Then, they vote to bury some of the heavy gold and jewels on the island. They do not want it to weigh them down when they attack another ship.

Bury the treasure!

The captain picks a few trustworthy pirates to row ashore in a small boat and bury the treasure. With shovels and pickaxes, they dig a deep hole and lower in the loot.

X *marks the spot!*

The pirates carefully draw a map of the
exact spot where they buried the treasure.

Marooned!

Pirates take their rules, the Articles, very seriously. At their meeting, they voted to punish a pirate who broke the rules by keeping extra treasure for himself. They decided to maroon him on a tiny, barren island. After burying their treasure, the pirates row to a rocky islet, where they leave the doomed rule-breaker. If he is lucky, another ship will come by and pick him up. But the chances are that he will stay there a long, long time.

Pirate feast!

With the food taken from the merchant vessel, the cook has made a special pirate treat of salmagundi.

Anchors aweigh!

The crew is now ready to sail onward. It takes about twenty pirates to work the capstan. To help themselves push and pull together, they sing work songs or chanteys.

Good night, pirates!

As the ship sails into the dark sea, the night watch takes over, and the rest of the crew finish cleaning their guns and knives so they are ready for another day. The pirates are very tired. As they sway in their hammocks, the waves rock them to sleep.

Famous Pirates in History

Mary Read and Anne Bonney

Nearly all pirates were men—with some notable exceptions. Mary Read and Anne Bonney were two women who disguised themselves as men and became pirates. They were better sailors than most of the men on their ships. Mary was a young Englishwoman who ran away to find adventure. Anne went to sea when she fell in love with the famous pirate Calico Jack Rackham. She soon decided to become a pirate, too. Mary and Anne met when Mary's ship attacked a merchant ship on which Anne was hiding. Together, the two women terrorized the Caribbean until they were captured near Jamaica in 1720.

Blackbeard

Edward Teach, better known as Blackbeard, started his career as a pirate on Captain Benjamin Hornigold's ship in the Bahamas. He soon became more daring and ruthless than his teacher. In 1716, he set out on his own and terrified sailors from the Caribbean to Virginia. He was a huge man and got his name from his enormous black beard. He wore it tied up in little bunches with ribbons. He was finally killed by British lieutenant Robert Maynard at Ocracoke Inlet, North Carolina, on November 22, 1718.

Captain Kidd

After leaving his native Scotland at a young age, William Kidd became a privateer. In 1695, King William III of Great Britain ordered Kidd to catch several pirates who were causing trouble in the Indian Ocean and the Red Sea. After a year without capturing any new supplies, Kidd's crew threatened to mutiny. To keep his crew from getting out of hand, Kidd captured and pillaged a small Indian merchant ship. Before long, Kidd and his crew were robbing more ships than the pirates were! The king ordered Kidd arrested, and in 1701 he was hanged in London.

Black Bart

Bartholomew Roberts, known as Black Bart, was one of the most successful pirates in history. In just four years, he robbed over four hundred ships. He sailed wherever there was treasure. Roberts was born in Wales in 1682 and became a pirate when another pirate captain took him prisoner. Besides his courage and skill, Black Bart was known for his strictness on his ship. He made his crew stay quiet at night and held church services on Sundays. He was killed in 1722 by British captain Chaloner Ogle off the coast of West Africa.

Famous Pirates in Stories

Captain Hook

Captain Hook is the villain of James Matthew Barrie's story *Peter Pan*. He wears a metal hook in place of the hand that Peter Pan cut off and threw to a crocodile. Hook and his pirates seek revenge on Peter Pan and his band of Lost Boys, and the crocodile follows Hook in search of another snack.

Long John Silver

This mysterious pirate appears in *Treasure Island* by Robert Louis Stevenson, published in 1883. Long John Silver is an old pirate who is hired as the ship's cook on a voyage in search of buried treasure. With his crutch and his parrot, he has been the model for pirates in hundreds of stories.

Glossary

Articles: Written laws governing a ship's crew.

Boarding axes: Large, long-handled weapons used to board an enemy ship.

Capstan: The heavy wooden cylinder used to wind the rope that holds the anchor.

Captain: The officer in charge of a ship.

Compass: A magnetic device for determining direction.

Cross-staff: An instrument used in navigation to measure angles and the altitude of the sun and stars.

Crow's nest: A small platform high on a mast used as a lookout.

Cutlasses: Short, curved swords used by sailors.

Deck: The floor of a ship.

Fife: A small flute.

Galleons: Sailing ships of the fifteenth through eighteenth centuries often used by Spaniards to carry treasure and goods for trade.

Grappling hooks: Hooks used to fasten, or grapple, one ship to another.

Gunners: Strong sailors in charge of firing a ship's heavy cannons or guns.

Halyards: Lines or ropes used to raise a ship's sails.

Hold: The area of a ship where the cargo is stored.

Hornpipe: A wind instrument and the lively dance performed to its music.

Inlet: A small bay or recess in the shore.

Jolly Roger: A black flag with a white skull and crossbones often flown by pirate ships.

Latitude: North-south position of a ship relative to the equator.

Loot: Valuable goods taken by force.

Maroon: To leave alone on a deserted island or coast.

Masts: Tall poles or posts that support a ship's sails.

Mate: A helper or assistant to a more experienced sailor, or a fellow member of a ship's crew.

Merchant: A buyer and seller, or trader, of goods.

Muskets: Long-barreled guns fired from the shoulder.

Mutiny: Revolt by a ship's crew against its captain or officers.

Plank: Pirates often punish those who misbehave by making them walk off the end of a board or plank suspended over the sea.

Plunder: To rob or steal by force.

Powder monkeys: Young pirates, often only ten or twelve years old, who help the gunners.

Privateer: A "legal" pirate working for the government.

Pumps: Devices used to keep a ship from filling with water.

Quadrant: An instrument used for measuring the altitude of the sun and stars to aid navigation.

Quartermaster: A senior officer of a ship.

Ratlines: Tarred ropes that form the steps of a ship's rope ladders.

Recruit: A new member of a ship's crew.

Rigging: A system of lines or ropes that control the sails.

Salmagundi: A stew made from any of a variety of ingredients. It can include fish, crab, beef, pigeons, wine, spices, anchovies, fruit, cabbage, garlic, hard-boiled eggs, and onions, with an oil-and-vinegar dressing.

Spyglass: A small, folding telescope.

Squall: A sudden, violent wind often accompanied by rain or snow.

Stinkpot: A jar filled with foul-smelling chemicals often thrown onto the deck of an enemy's ship.

Stores: Supplies of food, drink, and other provisions.

Vessel: A craft used for transportation in and on water.

Watch: A period of duty assigned to a sailor.

Yards: Wooden poles that support a ship's sails.

To Adam & Jud and all of the children who have touched our lives.
And thank you to Phyllis Danko and Linda Thompson
for their help with the research for this book
—J. T. and B. M.

To Charlie and Sean
—P. O.

Kenneth J. Kinkor, historical consultant

Text copyright © 1996 by Julie Thompson and Brownie Macintosh
Illustrations copyright © 1996 by Patrick O'Brien
All rights reserved, including the right of reproduction
in whole or in part in any form.

Published by Charlesbridge Publishing
85 Main Street, Watertown, MA 02472 • (617) 926-0329
www.charlesbridge.com

Library of Congress Cataloging-in-Publication Data
Thompson, Julie.
A pirate's life for me!: a day aboard a pirate ship / by Julie Thompson and
Brownie Macintosh; illustrated by Patrick O'Brien.
p. cm.
Summary: Describes life aboard a pirate ship and provides
information about famous pirates in history and literature.
ISBN 0-88106-932-9 (reinforced for library use)
ISBN 0-88106-931-0 (softcover)
1. Pirates—Juvenile literature. [1. Pirates.] I. Macintosh, Brownie.
II. O'Brien, Patrick, 1960– ill. III. Title.
G535.M218   1996   95-36169
910.4'5—dc20

Printed in the United States of America
(hc) 10 9 8 7 6 5 4 3 2
(sc) 10 9 8 7 6 5 4

The illustrations in this book were done in Alkyd oil paints
on Arches watercolor paper.
The display type and text type were set in Opti Caslon Antique
and Galliard by Diane M. Earley.
Color separations were made by Pure Imaging, Watertown, Massachusetts.
Printed and bound by Worzalla Publishing Company, Stevens Point, Wisconsin
This book was printed on recycled paper.
Production supervision by Brian G. Walker
Designed by Diane M. Earley